Published by Creative Education
123 South Broad Street, Mankato, Minnesota 56001
Creative Education is an imprint of The Creative Company

Art direction by Rita Marshall
Production design by The Design Lab

Library of Congress Cataloging-in-Publication Data

Frisch, Aaron.
Llamas / by Aaron Frisch.
p. cm. — (Let's investigate)
Summary: Presents information on llamas, including their physical
characteristics and behavior, as well as how people in South
America have utilized them throughout history.
ISBN 1-58341-242-5
1. Llamas—Juvenile literature. [1. Llamas.] I. Title. II. Series.
QL737.U54 F74   2002
599.63'67—dc21   2001047893

First edition

2 4 6 8 9 7 5 3 1

LLAMAS

AARON FRISCH

Creative Education

LLAMA
RUNNING

Llamas move gracefully and will sometimes break into a trot—simultaneously lifting both feet on the same side when running.

4

Llamas have adapted well to mountain life

The majestic Andes Mountains run for 4,500 miles (7,245 km) along the western edge of South America. For nearly as long as humans have traversed the valleys, **plateaus**, and peaks of these mountains, llamas have been at their sides. Known for their distinct build and docile nature, llamas have played numerous roles as domestic animals and worked their way into the lives and hearts of many people.

LLAMA
HOME

Llamas are the only beasts of burden native to the Western Hemisphere. Cattle, horses, donkeys, and other animals were brought to the Americas from lands overseas.

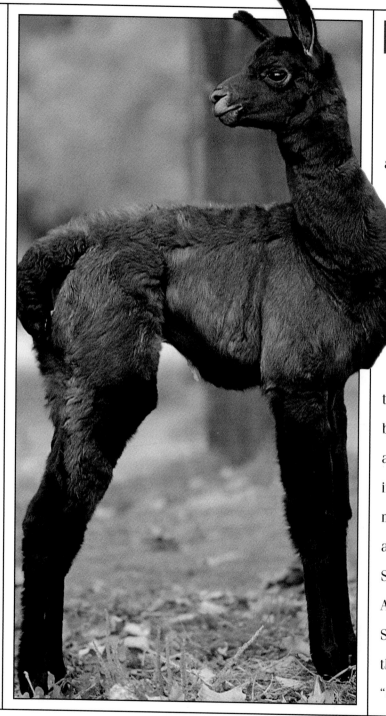

A baby llama, called a cria

CAMELID EVOLUTION

Not long after dinosaurs became extinct, a mammal about the size of a jackrabbit **evolved** on the plains of what is now the United States. Two to three million years ago, some of these animals made their way across a land bridge between Alaska and Asia and developed into camels. Others moved south and settled along the west coast of South America in the Andes Mountains. Scientists today refer to these animals as "camelids."

*Llamas are so closely related to alpacas, guanacos, and vicuñas that members of different species can interbreed and produce **fertile** offspring.*

S ince its prehistoric **migration**, the camelid has evolved into four separate but very closely related species. There is the guanaco (*Lama guanicoe*), a fleet-footed animal that dwells in the foothills and lower plateaus of the Andes; the vicuña (*Lama vicugna*), a small, shy species that lives at high, cold elevations; the alpaca (*Lama pacos*), a gentle animal known for its silky coat; and the llama (*Lama glama*), the largest and strongest of the four species.

A herd of alpacas

LLAMA

RELATIVE

Alpacas, which look like small, shaggy llamas, are bred for their fine coats. The animals have 22 natural coat colors that can be either solid or mixed.

**Above, the wooly head of an alpaca
Right, a llama**

Scientists are not sure of the exact relationship between the camelids, but many believe that the guanaco and vicuña developed first, and that the llama and alpaca came into existence about 5,000 years ago when people began to domesticate and **breed** the wild camelids. The guanaco and vicuña have remained wild through-out their history, but domesticated llamas and alpacas have lived alongside people for thousands of years.

THE LITTLE CAMELS

Early in the 16th century, **conquistadors** from Spain arrived on the west coast of South America. The natives of that region kept hundreds of thousands of llamas for their coats, meat, and use as pack animals. Noting the resemblance between the llamas and the larger camels of the Eastern Hemisphere, the Spaniards called llamas the "little camels of the Andes."

Although llamas are good pack animals, they move at their own pace and won't be hurried by shouting or prodding.

Specially designed backpacks help llamas move goods easily

L L A M A

Llamas are quiet animals. They communicate mainly through facial expressions, body posturing, groaning, and humming.

A llama's features closely resemble those of a camel

Because they evolved from the same prehistoric animal, llamas and camels do share many characteristics. Like camels, llamas have long, thin legs and a long neck. Also like camels, llamas have a split upper lip, as well as long lashes that protect their large eyes.

LLAMA
MYSTERY

*For reasons un-
known, llamas have
the peculiar habit
of facing the sun at
sunrise and emitting
groans at sunset.*

L lamas are the biggest of the camelids, standing about four feet (1.2 m) at the shoulder and weighing between 250 and 350 pounds (114–159 kg). Their large size, good physical endurance, and unique foot structure—two toes with a large, leathery pad on the bottom of the foot—make them excellent pack animals, which has been their primary use throughout history. Llamas measure about six feet (1.8 m) tall at the head, and they seem to gaze down at the people and animals around them with a snobbish facial expression.

A llama family

LLAMA
DIET

Llamas need relatively little food and water. A 300-pound (136 kg) llama needs about six pounds (2.7 kg) of dry food and three gallons (11.4 l) of water per day.

Llamas feed on an array of vegetation that includes grass, leaves, moss, and **lichen**. Llamas and their relatives have three-chambered stomachs and are ruminants, which means that they chew their food, swallow it, and then **regurgitate** it to chew again. This process allows llamas to go for several days before eating again if necessary.

An alpaca and a llama grazing on grass

13

Llamas are generally good-natured animals that are easy to work with and handle. However, if they think they have worked long enough or if their load is too heavy, they will kneel or lie down and refuse to move. If a llama gets especially irritated or feels threatened, it will raise its head, draw foul-smelling saliva from its first stomach chamber, and spit in the face of its antagonist. This is a unique skill that all camelids have.

Once tired, llamas can be stubborn and difficult to move

LLAMA
TRAVEL

The Empress Josephine, wife of French dictator Napoleon Bonaparte, had a mixed group of 36 camelids shipped to France around 1800. All of the animals died.

Llamas thrive in the rugged mountains of South America

LLAMA BIOLOGY

Most llamas live in Bolivia, but they are also raised in the mountains of Peru, Argentina, and Chile. Llamas may live at elevations of up to 16,000 feet (4,878 m). This high in the mountains, there is much less oxygen available than there is at sea level. To live in these conditions, llamas and other camelids have unusually large lungs and hearts. These specialized organs—as well as **hemoglobin** that absorbs high

amounts of oxygen—enable llamas and their relatives to live at elevations that few other animals can tolerate.

LLAMA
SYMBOL

The llama and the wild vicuña adorn Peru's coat of arms (national symbol) and many of its people's crafts.

LLAMA
RELATIVE

A grown alpaca produces about four pounds (1.8 kg) of fiber each year; one ounce (28 g) can sell for three to six U.S. dollars.

LLAMA
ROLLING

Llamas spend a lot of time rolling on the ground, usually in bare spots of dirt. This helps them fluff up their coats and maintain their insulation.

A display of llama coat coloration

The long, dense coats of llamas can be one color or multicolored and appear in many shades of brown, gray, black, and white. Like all camelids, llamas have a coat that consists of outer guard hairs and a down undercoat. The guard hairs, which make up about 20 percent of the coat, are thick, straight, and wiry, and protect the animal from wind and rain. The soft, short down hairs—the part of the coat that may be spun for fabric—insulate llamas from the cold.

Llamas usually live 15 to 20 years, and females are capable of reproducing for the first time when they are between one and two years old. Females are pregnant for about 11 months before giving birth to a single baby called a cria (though they occasionally have twins). Within a half-hour of birth, the crias can run and follow their mothers. Llamas are herd animals and like to be with others of their kind. They can adapt to living with other kinds of livestock, but they become unhappy when kept alone.

A female llama and her cria

In the 15th century, the mighty Inca Empire in the Andes Mountains of modern-day Peru was at the peak of its power. With a population of between 5 and 10 million people, a 9,300-mile (15,000 km) system of roads, a powerful army, and elegant architecture, this empire was truly one of the world's most marvelous achievements—one that never would have existed without the llama.

LLAMA
GEOGRAPHY

Fossil evidence suggests that llamas were first domesticated near Lake Titicaca on the border between Peru and Bolivia.

19

The llama played a key role in building the ancient city of Machu Picchu

LLAMA

PRODUCTS

Llama fiber can be made into a variety of products. These include hats, rugs, scarves, jackets, blankets, sandals, fishing flies, and backpacks.

Above, goods made of woven llama fiber
Right, a llama loaded with grain

The llama was most valuable to the mountain-dwelling Incas as a pack animal. By loading packs of between 50 and 100 pounds (23–45 kg) onto the backs of llamas, workers could transport tools and materials as far as 20 miles (32 km) a day, allowing the Incas to construct elaborate networks of roads and **irrigation** systems.

Vicuñas have been widely slaughtered for their silky wool. By the 1960s, when they became protected by law, a population of millions had been reduced to 15,000.

21

T he llama, as well as the wild guanaco, was also responsible for clothing the peasant population of the empire. The Incas were masterful weavers of camelid fiber, creating all types of garments from the animals' coats. The Incan emperor and his nobles, however, were above wearing the rather coarse fabric of llamas. This elite class wore only the best robes and shawls woven from the finer wool of the domestic alpaca or the silky fiber of the wild vicuña.

A woman weaving dyed alpaca wool

LLAMA
VALUE

In the Inca Empire, llamas were so valuable that they were considered the property of the empire. Llama herders were considered members of nobility and were paid very well.

A Peruvian man wearing a llama-wool poncho

After llamas reached 10 or 12 years of age—too old to carry pack loads—they were butchered. When a llama was killed, nothing went to waste: all meat was eaten, all usable wool was taken, and the bones were carved into spoons, needles, flutes, beads, or ornaments.

In one Incan ritual, a black llama was symbolically loaded with the sins of the empire and driven into the mountains, thereby cleansing the empire.

The Incas believed that llamas were sacred to the gods, and the animals were sacrificed by the hundreds for many reasons: to diagnose disease, forecast the outcomes of wars, and test the truth of confessions. Llamas of specific colors were sacrificed to different gods, although animals with the same colored coat and muzzle—particularly pure white or black—were thought to be the most acceptable offerings.

The Incas sometimes sacrificed brown llamas to the gods

LLAMA
SACRIFICE

Peruvians still sacrifice one white llama each year at Lake Titicaca as a prayer for good crops.

I n one ritual, a pure white llama was designated as the holiest of animals. Early in the Incan year, this sacred llama—called the *Napa*—was brought to Cuzco, the capital city of the empire. The animal was dressed in a red robe, adorned with golden ear ornaments, and paraded by its own attendants. The llama, which represented the first llama on Earth, enjoyed pampered treatment until its death, at which time a successor was carefully selected.

Sacrificed white llamas were thought to bring good fortune

LLAMA
DANGERS

Pumas and foxes kill many young camelids, and the Andean condor—a gigantic bird that lives at very high altitudes—sometimes feeds on small vicuñas.

LLAMA
TRANSPORT

Though they are still used as pack animals in the most rugged parts of the Andes, llamas have largely been replaced by trucks as a means of transport.

A llama in the Andes Mountains, once home to the Inca Empire

THE VERSATILE BEASTS

The Inca Empire's culture, religion, and way of life all came to a violent end with the arrival of the Spanish conquistadors. In 1533, the invaders, led by Francisco Pizarro, murdered the Incan emperor Atahuallpa and soon overran the empire. The Spaniards—mounted on horses and carrying guns—slaughtered many llamas and much of the native population.

LLAMA
RELIC

In the ancient Incan city of Machu Picchu, scientists have unearthed a huge sacrifice table in the shape of a llama.

The bond between Peruvians and llamas is thousands of years old

Although the mighty Inca Empire was completely destroyed just decades after the invasion, descendants of that lost tribe continue to rely on llamas and their relatives today. About half of Peru's population are descendants of the Incas. Like their ancestors, these Peruvians depend on the llama's carrying strength and warm fiber in everyday life.

The surefooted llama (pronounced "yama" in South America) continues to be used as a pack animal and a source of food by many villagers in the **altiplano** region of the Andes. A single llama can produce 7 to 18 pounds (3.2–8.2 kg) of spinnable fiber every two years, and native people still make clothing and rope from the hair. Llama **tallow** is used to make candles, and the animals' excrement is used both as fuel and crop fertilizer.

A woman separating sheared llama wool into spinnable fibers

LLAMA
RELATIVE

Alpaca fibers—which are either sheared or taken from the animals with heavy brushes—are hollow, making alpaca-wool garments very warm yet lightweight.

LLAMA
GOLFING

People continue to find new uses for llamas. In recent years, some llamas have even appeared on golf courses as caddies.

Llamas can handle rough, uneven mountain trails with ease

Llamas were first brought to North America about 100 years ago. Today, llamas can be found throughout the United States and Canada. Llamas are hardy and adaptable animals that are inexpensive to raise. In addition to providing wool, llamas are used as pack animals for recreational activities such as backpacking and hiking. They are especially useful in delicate environmental

tal areas, since their soft, padded feet do not dig into the earth the way that horse and mule hooves can. Many people also enjoy raising llamas as pets or for show in judging competitions.

LLAMA
MOVIE

A llama is the central character in the 2000 animated Disney movie The Emperor's New Groove. *In the film, a young emperor named Kuzco is poisoned and turned into a llama.*

LLAMA
COURAGE

Llamas used as guard animals in North America have been seen threatening moose that were passing by the llamas' pasture.

LLAMA
ENEMIES

*Llamas have a natural dislike for **canines**. Llamas kept as guard animals can stomp to death a dog or coyote that won't retreat when warned.*

Ranchers driving a herd of llamas through the mountains

Farmers and ranchers have discovered that llamas also make excellent livestock guardians, especially of sheep. The best guardian is a single **gelded** male around two years old. At this age, the llama is old enough to be territorial, but young enough to adopt its new "family." Guard llamas assume leadership of the flock and protect their territory—usually a pasture or meadow. They will position themselves between a predator and the flock, chasing and biting at the intruder to drive it away.

With its fluffy coat, long eyelashes, smirking expression, and often peculiar behavior, the llama has become an endearing pet for many people in recent years. But its strength, intelligence, and gentle disposition as a beast of burden are the qualities that have made it most useful to people throughout history. After existing alongside humans for more than 4,000 years, the llama continues to find new ways to fit into the lives of people on two continents.

LLAMA GUARDS

Llamas can be effective guardians of sheep, ducks, geese, deer, and cattle. A good guard llama typically costs between 500 and 1,200 U.S. dollars.

Glossary

An **altiplano** is a high plateau or plain, usually in a mountainous area.

People **breed** animals by putting a male and a female together to reproduce.

Canines are members of a mammal family that includes dogs, wolves, and coyotes.

Conquistadors were Spanish soldiers that came to conquer parts of Mexico and Peru in the 1500s.

Life forms that have undergone physical or biological change over many years have **evolved**.

A **fertile** animal is one that is able to produce offspring.

A **gelded** male llama is one whose reproductive organs have been removed.

Hemoglobin is a pigment in blood that helps carry oxygen from the lungs to the muscles.

Irrigation is the process of supplying crops with water through pipes or ditches.

Lichen are plants that grow on rocky ground in cool or mountainous areas.

Migration is the mass movement of animals from one region to another.

Flat areas of land at high elevations are known as **plateaus**.

Animals that **regurgitate** force partially digested food up from the stomach to the mouth.

Tallow is animal fat that can be made into candles, soap, and oil.

Zoologists are scientists who study animals and classify them into groups based on their biological characteristics.

Index

alpacas, 7, 8, 16, 21, 27
babies, *see crias*
bodies, 10–11, 14–15
breeding, 7, 18
butchering, 22
camelids, 6–8

coats, 8, 16
  fiber, 20, 21, 27
communication, 10
crias, 18
enemies, 25
evolution, 6–8
feeding, 12

feet, 11, 29
fossils, 19
guanacos, 7, 8, 21
guardians, llamas as, 30, 31
habitats, 4, 6, 14

hauling goods, 9, 20, 25, 28
Inca Empire, 19–26
Josephine, Empress, 14
life expectancy, 18

Napa, 24
running, 4
sacrifices, 23–24, 26
Spaniards, 9, 25
temper, 9, 13
vicuñas, 7, 8, 15, 21

Photographs by Affordable Photo Stock (Francis E. Caldwell), Jurgen Ankenbrand, Frank S. Balthis, Robert E. Barber, Corbis (EcoScene, Wolfgang Kaehler, Galen Rowell, Staffan Widstrand), The Image Finders (Jim Baron, Gary Leppart), JLM Visuals (Breck P. Kent), Alison M. Jones, Sally McCrae Kuyper, Gunter Marx Photography, Jeff Myers, John Perryman, James P. Rowan